Vet

Lucy M. George   Ando Twin

Mike the vet lives in the countryside.
He looks after lots of animals such as
cows, horses, sheep and pigs.

Today Mike is working at the surgery.
Suddenly the phone rings!

"RRRIIIINNGG!!!"

It's Gillian, the farmer.
One of her animals
is in trouble!

There's a storm outside.
The big wheels of Mike's car splash
down the muddy lane to the farm.

Gillian meets Mike at the gate.

"This way!" she shouts over the wind, pointing to the field. "One of my sheep is having trouble giving birth to her lamb!"

They reach the ewe just in time. Mike kneels down in the mud to take a closer look.

"Pass my bag please, Gillian!" Mike calls. "I think the lamb is stuck!"

In the warm barn, Mike helps the ewe give birth to her lamb. The lamb is safe!

Just then, they hear a voice calling, "Mum!"

It's Megan, Gillian's daughter. Her dog is trapped.

"One of Prince's legs is
stuck in the chicken run!
Come quickly." cries Megan.

Prince is very upset. "Shh, boy, it's okay,"
Mike says gently.

Mike is very good with animals, and Prince calms down.

Mike frees Prince's paw quickly
and looks at his leg. Megan
strokes Prince's head.

"Poor boy!" she says.

Prince has hurt himself, so they take him back
to the surgery. He is going to need a bandage.

Mike opens his vet bag, washes his hands and puts on his gloves.

He cleans the wound and puts a bandage on Prince's leg. "There you go, Prince. All better!" he says.

The next day, Mike goes back to Gillian's farm to visit the lambs.

He checks on the new lamb and makes sure all the others are healthy.

While he is at the farm, Mike checks the other animals too. He visits the pigs...

...and the horses.

Then Mike examines the cows. He checks their hooves, eyes, tongues and udders. All the animals look happy and healthy.

Finally, Mike and Gillian go into the warm farmhouse. They are having tea when...

...Prince bounds into the kitchen!

His leg is much better and he's very happy to see Mike.

"WOOF!"

What else does Mike do?

Examines sick animals in the surgery.

Operates on animals.

Gives vaccinations.

Tests samples in the lab.

What does Mike need?

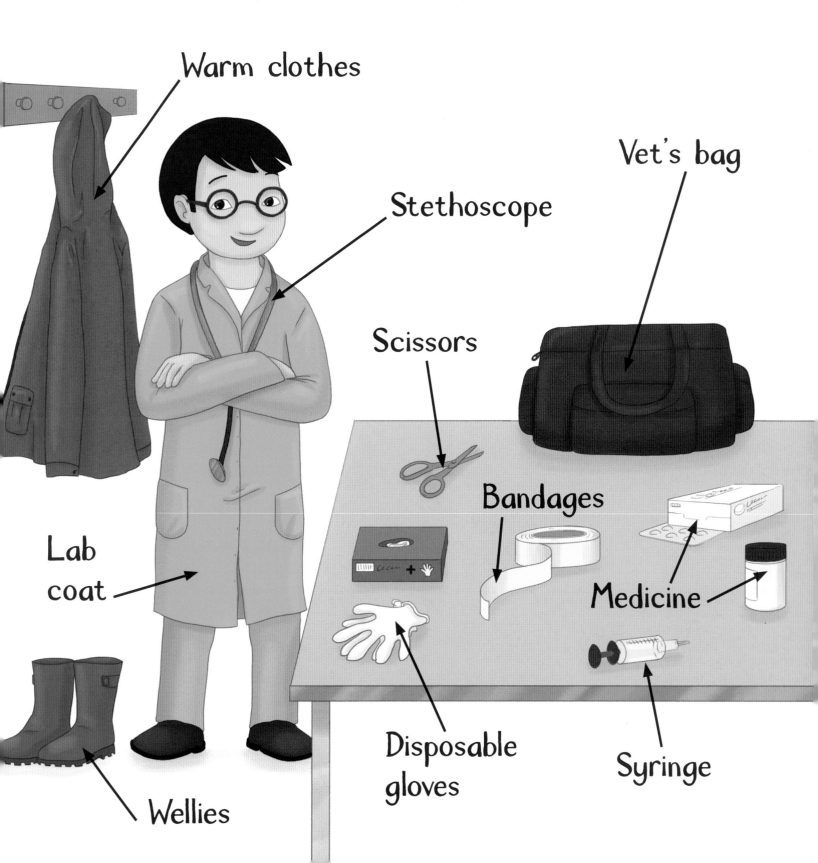

Warm clothes

Stethoscope

Vet's bag

Scissors

Bandages

Medicine

Lab coat

Disposable gloves

Syringe

Wellies

Other busy people

Here are some of the other busy people vets work with.

Farmers breed and look after lots of animals – sometimes thousands! Each and every animal needs to be kept happy and healthy.

Animal rescue workers care for pets that have been lost or neglected. They also look after wild animals that are ill or injured.

Zookeepers feed and care for many different types of animal from all over the world. They make sure that the animals are healthy and call a vet if there are any problems.

Veterinary nurses work in a vet's surgery caring for sick animals.

Next steps

- Ask the children whether they have ever met a vet. Do they have any pets? Discuss with the children what animals need to stay healthy and how we can help take care of them.

- Have any of the children visited a farm? Discuss what animals they saw there. Do the children have a favourite animal?

- Discuss the animals Mike saw in the book and how he helped each of them. Would any of the children like to be a vet? What would they like or find difficult about the job?

- Think about the equipment Mike needs for his work. Why does he need each of the items shown in this book?

- Talk about the other busy people vets work with. Discuss their different jobs and what they might involve. Which job would the children like to do most? What kinds of animals would the children like to work with?

Publisher: Zeta Jones
Associate Publisher: Maxime Boucknooghe
Editorial Director: Victoria Garrard
Art Director: Laura Roberts-Jensen
Editor: Sophie Hallam
Designer: Anna Lubecka

Copyright © QED Publishing 2015

First published in the UK in 2015 by
QED Publishing
Part of The Quarto Group,
The Old Brewery,
6 Blundell Street,
London, N7 9BH

www.qed-publishing.co.uk

A catalogue record for this book is available from the British Library.

ISBN 978 1 78493 147 6

Printed in China

**For Granny Wilson
- AndoTwin**

**For Leander, Finn & Rosie
- Lucy M. George**